Charge into Reading

Decodable Reader
with literacy activities

S blends

Stan and the Slug
S Blends

Brooke Vitale • Mila Uvarova

CHARGE MOMMY
BOOKS
Riverside, CT

Copyright © 2023 Charge Mommy Books, LLC. All rights reserved.

No part of this book may be reproduced or transmitted in any form or by any means, electronic or mechanical, including photocopying, recording, or by any information storage and retrieval system, without written permission from the publisher.

For information address contact@chargemommybooks.com
or visit chargemommybooks.com

Library of Congress Control Number: 2023904148

Printed in China
ISBN 978-1-955947-35-0
10 9 8 7 6

Designed by Lindsay Broderick
Created in consultation with literacy specialist Marisa Ware, MSEd

Stan can spin.
He spins and spins.

Stan can stomp.
He stomps and stomps.

Stan can skip.
He skips and skips.

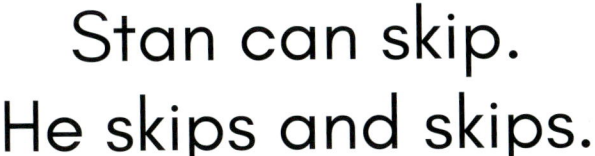

Stan slips.

He skids into a step.

Stan skins his leg.

Stan slumps on the step.
He sobs.

His sobs stop.
A slug is on the step.

Stan taps the slug.
The slug slips into
a gap in the step.

Stan stands up.
He scans the slab.

Stan spots a stem.
He slips the stem into the gap.

The slug snags the stem.

The slug slips onto Stan.

Stan grins.
Slugs!

Let's Talk Literacy!

Read the sentence below. Then circle the picture that matches the sentence.

Stan spins and spins.

Let's Talk Literacy!

Each of the words below contains an S blend. Sound out each word. Then draw a line from **each word** to its **matching picture**.

nest   sled   slug   stem   swan   wasp

Let's Talk Literacy!

Say the name of each picture below. Then circle the words that contain an **S blend**.

Answers: stem, star, slide, slug, skunk

Let's Talk Literacy!

Read each word below. Then circle the pictures in each row that have names beginning with the same **initial consonant blend**.

skit

snap

spin

Answers: skunk, skull / snail, snake / spider, sponge

Let's Talk Literacy!

Say the name of each picture below. Then circle the correct **initial consonant blend** for each word.

sl sp st   sm st sw   sl sn sp

sc sl sp   sc sl sp   sl sp st

Answers: stick, swan, snail, spider, slug, star

Let's Talk Literacy!

Write the letters that form each picture word in the boxes below. Then draw a **scoop mark** under each consonant blend.

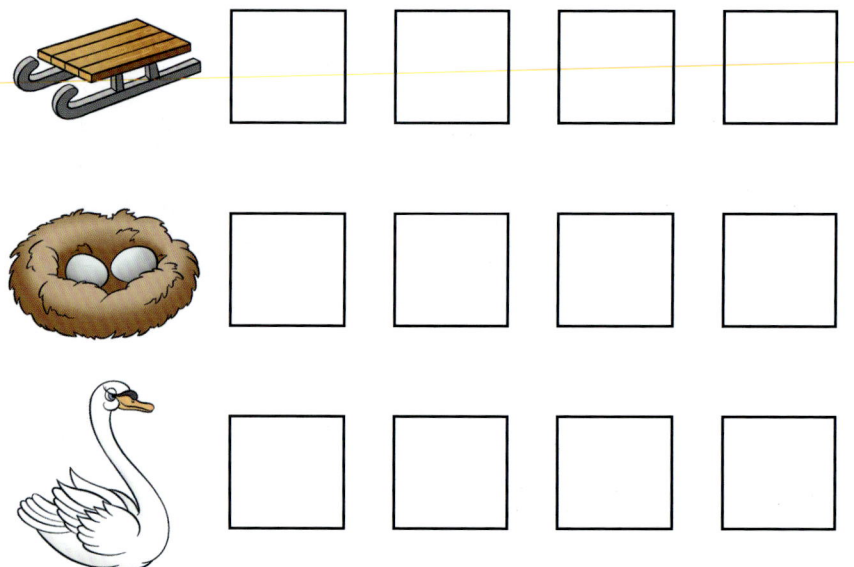

Answers: s-l-e-d / n-e-s-t / s-w-a-n

Let's Talk Literacy!

The name of each picture below contains a different consonant blend. Sort the words in the **word bank** by putting them under the picture of the word that uses the **same consonant blend**.

gasp	snug	slid	slam
rest	spot	snip	step

_____ _____ _____ _____

_____ _____ _____ _____

Let's Talk Literacy!

Say the name of each picture below. Then write the word's **initial consonant blend** on the line below the picture. The first one has been done for you.

__st__ _____ _____ _____

_____ _____ _____ _____

Answers: stop, swan, snail, sloth, slide, spider, star, slippers